THE BLIND STITCH

D1113549

ALSO BY GREG DELANTY

Poetry

The Hellbox

American Wake

Southward

Cast in the Fire

Special Editions

The Fifth Province

Striped Ink

Translations

Aristophanes, *The Suits*

Euripides, *Orestes*

Edited Volumes

Jumping Off Shadows: Selected
Contemporary Irish Poets
(with Nuala Ní Dhomhnaill)

The Selected Poems of Patrick Galvin
(with Robert Welch)

THE · BLIND · STITCH

POEMS ✷ GREG DELANTY

Louisiana State ⅂Ⅼ University Press
Baton Rouge

Copyright © 2002 by Greg Delanty
All rights reserved
Manufactured in the United States of America
First printing
Cloth: 5 4 3 2 1   Paper: 5 4 3 2 1
11 10 09 08 07 06 05 04 03 02   11 10 09 08 07 06 05 04 03 02

Designer: Laura Roubique Gleason
Typeface: Janson Text
Printer and binder: Thomson-Shore, Inc.

ISBN 0-8071-2820-1 (cloth); ISBN 0-8071-2821-X (paper)

For the Irish slang and other words, see Bernard Share's *Slanguage: A Dictionary of Irish Slang* (Dublin: Gill & Macmillan, 1997) and Seán Beecher's *A Dictionary of Cork Slang* (Cork: Goldy Angel Press, 1983). Some translations of Irish words in the poems are alphabetically as follows: a chara: my friend; an bhriogáid dóiteáin: the fire brigade; brostaigh: hurry; dán (pronounced *dawn*): poetry, craft, gift, offering, calling; fear gorm: fear means man, gorm means blue (coloured people were often called blue, probably because of the blue tint in some people's skin); leaba: bed; mála: bag; máthair: mother; rince: dance; Sasanach: the English; Siúl na Lobhar: Siúl means walk, Lobhar is pronounced *lover* but means leper; Táim trí thine: I'm on fire. The Hindi word angrezi means foreigner.

For the life of Father Damien, see John Farrow's *Damien the Leper* (New York: Doubleday, 1998). Father Damien (1849–99) was a missionary priest on the island of Molokai from 1873 until his death from leprosy. He realized that he had contracted leprosy when he spilled boiling water on himself and felt nothing. A symptom of the disease is anesthesia of nerves. The epigraph to "The Scalding," which translates as "In this place there is no law," was the informal motto of lepers on the island. The scientific name for leprosy is *Mycobacterium leprae*. In "450°" the final syllable of *connishur* is a full rhyme with *more*. The pledge is to take an oath to abstain from alcohol. In "The Malayalam Box," Bewley's is a renowned Dublin café. Recently it has opened franchises in other Irish cities, including Cork. The epigraph translation to "The Leper and Civil Disobedience" comes from Seán Connolly, "Vita Prima Sanctae Brigitae: Background and Historical Value," *Journal of the Royal Society of Antiquaries of Ireland* 119 (1989).

This book was published in Ireland and Great Britain by Oxford *Poets*, Carcanet, in 2001.

The paper in this book meets the guidelines for permanence and durability of the Committee on Production Guidelines for Book Longevity of the Council on Library Resources. ♾

AKNOWLEDGMENTS

Thanks go to the editors of the following publications, in which some of the poems herein first appeared, sometimes in slightly different form: *Atlantic Monthly, Boston College Magazine, Cork Review, Green Mountain Review, The Independent on Sunday, The Irish Review, The Irish Times, Kenyon Review, New Hibernia, The New Republic, Pequod, PN Review, Poetry Ireland Review, Prairie Schooner, Rattapallax, Shenandoah, The Shop, Southern Review, TriQuarterly.*

"Behold the Brahmany Kite" was a prizewinner in the National Poetry Competition, sponsored by The Poetry Society, England. "Tagging the Stealer" appeared in the *Atlantic Monthly*, 1997. "The Bindi Mirror" appeared in the *Atlantic Monthly*, 2000. "The Blind Stitch" first appeared in *The Norton Introduction to Poetry*, Eighth Edition (New York: W. W. Norton, 2002). "The Stilt Fisherman" first appeared in *Poets of the New Century*, ed. Roger Weingarten and Richard M. Higgerson (Boston: David R. Godine, 2001). "The Emerald Isle, Sri Lanka" first appeared in *Human Rights Have No Borders: Voices of Irish Poets*, ed. Kenneth Morgan and Almut Schlepper (Dublin: Marino Books, 1998).

The author gratefully acknowledges the support of the Arts Council/An Chomhairle Ealaíon, Dublin, Ireland; The Wolfer-O'Neill Literary Foundation; and The Royal Literary Fund.

CONTENTS

CONTENTS

CONTENTS

THE BLIND STITCH

The Scalding

'A'ole kanawai ma keia wahi!

Long past lights-out I pored over *Lives of the Saints*
       with my Woolworth's torch as others read *The Rover,*
Wizard or *Wonder Woman,* unafraid of sacrificing my sight,
       albeit I feared blindness zealously performing Onan.
I preached to gulls from the Blackash, lip-read goldfish,
       yapped with stray cats and dogs. After my nature project
collaged the minute-by-minute extinction of plants,
       animals and birds, I switched to the other Francis
like a football fan who divines his star is over the hill.
       As Francis Xavier, my uncorrupted body returned to
the Goa of Cork, and the city flocked round my glass coffin.
       But my real idol, even if he was in the halfpenny
venerable league, was the leper lover, Damien of Molokai.

                                        *

Never one for half measures, I prayed to be a Damien, exile
       among exiles, giving succour and mending the wanton ways
of the living dead, men and women dulling their plight, losing
       themselves in what was glossed as bodily whims
that secretly had us all curiously, if only dimly, envious.
       In preparation for my island I trained myself to bear
the walking dead's putrefying stench, taking deep breaths
       when Alex Casey slipped off his shoes beneath the desk.
I held tough as the whole Palace shrank from lepers in *Ben Hur.*
       The terror thrilled as we gasped at sackcloth creatures
with noseless faces, suppurating eyes, and stumps for hands.
       They grovelled out of caves darker than the confessional,

their bell-ringing scarier than a Monday morning school bell.
     I pestered my mother for sewing tips, intent as Damien
to dignify lepers and outfit a band to accompany funerals,
          fashioning drums, pipes and fifes from rusty kerosene cans.
Musicians, often missing three or four fingers, miraculously
          turned into maestros, backed by the harmony of sea and surf.

*

A school missionary told us the story: how the leper priest
          mistakenly poured boiling water on his flesh and, feeling no
pain, smiled and nodded to himself. The carried-away padre
          addressed the class congregation, as Damien addressed
his flock next morning, almost joyously, with "We lepers."
     He spoke of another strain—name it *Macrobacterium leprae*—
the bacilli of complicity carried in our food and clothes,
          in hidden seams of our varied regular lives, sewn by
the world's less fortunate hands, unseen as Molokai's lepers;
          how really we're all lepers, even if we are dismissive,
like that dame who, as Damien stepped onto the island, cut off
          her finger, turned her back and flung the finger over
her shoulder. The priest surveyed us querying: "Do we nod
          and smile to ourselves? Have we spilled the scalding water?"
He exhorted us to go out, hereafter, into the world as Damiens.

*

Barmy as it sounds, I never quite shook off that sermon, but feel,
    at best, like Damo's crotchety attendant
watching the pot bubble on the stove, tired of being kept late,
    setting the steaming kettle down before I sign off.

To My Mother, Eileen

I'm threading the eye
    of the needle for you again. That is
my specially appointed task, my
        gift that you gave me. Ma, watch me slip this
        camel of words through. Yes,
rich we are still even if your needlework
    has long since gone with the rag-and-bone man
        and Da never came home one day, our Dan.
Work Work Work. Lose yourself in work.
    That's what he'd say.
        Okay okay.
Ma, listen I can hear the sticks of our fire spit
    like corn turning into popcorn
        with the brown insides of rotten teeth. We sit
in our old Slieve Mish house. Norman is just born.
    He's in the pen.
I raise the needle to the light and lick the thread
        to stiffen the limp words. I
peer through the eye, focus and put everything out of my head.
        I shut my right eye and thread.
I'm important now, a likely lad, instead
    of the amadán at Dread School. I have the eye
        haven't I, the knack?
    I'm Prince Threader. I missed it that try.
        Concentrate. Concentrate. Enough yackety yak.
There, there, Ma, look, here's the threaded needle back.

450°F

to Peggy Kenneally

Peg of the swan-white hair, I'm word-stretched to give you
Your due, queenmáthair of givers, never wanting more
Than a quiet chat, no noodeenaw connishur,
And a cuppa Barry's cha with maybe a teaspoon or two
Of sweet slagging; how you've a fella hidden somewhere;
About breaking the Pledge when Joe, the last of your lot,
Your Mr. Bachelor Boy son himself, knots the knot
He's tying now; how he's sure to have *your* dessert there,
Your one treat: a sheer impossibility of frozen ice cream
Baked in an oven turned up high enough to sap a body,
Between layers of sponge cake and a frosting dream
Of meringue that crumbles as quickly as would everybody
Should anything happen to you. O Aunt Me Daza,
This is my half-baked, dished-up effort at Baked Alaska.

A Cork Prothalamium

for Joe Kenneally and Doris Flanagan

This is a day I'd love to sconce you in the black
    of a dressed-to-kill, one-day monkey suit
instead of the dressed-to-mourn shades of black
        we wear the odd occasion we now get to meet
        at the muted family get-together of a funeral.
But there'll be naught low-key about this day of days;
    you chucking tarry-boy ways; ducking the usual
ball-and-chain crack, twigging it ain't a leaba of roses,
        but that you would be out of your tree
    to let Doris, your jag, your gauzer, your lasher,
        slip by. Joe, I'd give anything to see
you both cut a scatter up the aisle and you, the masher,
        king of ballhoppers, confetti-showered in a benevolence
of slagging, finally getting your comeuppance.

*

Were I there, you'd be sure to razz me about that day
    you saved me from drowning in Redbarn;
you, our cozening coz, master of slagging's by-the-way,
        hop-the-ball play of affection.
But Jesus, for once I'll risk dropping the slag
    to openly say that I've great smack for you,
        how many a time you saved me from the drag
        of a dreary old Cork day—maybe bumping into
you on Blarney Street, or over a jorum—with your giddum.
So, from across the drink, this toasting prothalamium.

Homage to the God of Pollution in Brooklyn

The gravid grey sky, languor made visible, threatens rain, but holds
    back to keep us
on edge, wind-whispering—if winds could really whisper—what in
    vain we can't catch; call them
intimations of, call it the old country. But what's odd about this drear
    déjà vu is
what was once laden with melancholia, heebie-jeebies, willies, now
    seeps with comforting familiarity.

But this emigrant nostalgia run amuck has far less to do with the drab
    welkin
than the concomitant gray-green water of Brooklyn drifting into
    Buttermilk Channel and the waters
surrounding Ms. Liberty, befouling the hem of her dress.

Like so many, I grew up in a town with a belovèd river the colour of
    slime
I took for the natural colour of all waterways. I couldn't fathom why
    teachers made us paint
the waters of our colourbooks blue, and ever since, passing through
    cities,
I hardly think twice about why I've never beheld a winding blue
    streak even on sunny days.

And as much as I'm over the moon about rumors of this mire's clean
    up

and concur with the protesters crying for the waters, O Aqua Mundi;
    as much
as I want to see the waters swell like the fish-surging biblical sea of
    the miraculous catch,
a story I loved as a kid; as much as I'd give my writing arm to witness
    trees along the banks
shake off their sickly hue, and to hear returning birds of the
    resurrected world
hosanna the airways, I admit to a silent prayer perverse.

I confess to the god of pollution in Brooklyn that if ever this blue
    that frightens me to dwell on
can be retrieved, I'll be lonesome for the iniquity of fishless water
    slouching towards the putrid shore. But heaven
on earth, I don't suppose I need worry on that score.

Elegy for an Aunt

You'd not credit it, but tonight I lost my way and there wasn't a
    sinner to direct me
in the maze of alleys narrower than the lanes off Cork's norrie quays,
    and as manky,
when around one corner trots a funeral of Hindus with fanny-all on
    but their dhoti badinahs.

*

I stepped aside from pallbearers shouldering a tinsel-covered body
    about the size of Kitty's,
whose bier I bore only weeks ago onto Gurranabraher and the hills
    down to the Lee,
our Ganges, with its ghats of chemical factories.

I can still feel the dead weight imprinting my right shoulder and
    glimpse
taspy Joe out of badinage and a laugh, backed to the church
    wall.
We all copped another of the Old World souls was cut from us, as
    Rosy was and Noel and

and and, and with each *and* a subtraction as if we're disappearing
    ourselves
limb by phantom limb. Soon, I think, we'll be nothing but air.

As the dolorous bearers wound their way, it dawned on me, if I
    followed,
they'd lead me to my lodgings above the burning ghat. Trailing,
    I felt
like an aish who tags a funeral through streets at home for free drink.

I doubt I could have gone further from whatever home is under the
    embers of the Indian night
as I dekkoed a mourner scrawl the ash tilak of his dead before he
    swept the remains into
the heaven of the Ganges; the wherever of the hereafter.

*

Now monkeys lumber and loaf on the balcony outside my room
    above the cremation's glow.
I still smell of pall smoke and my eyes water as they strain
    to follow
my pencil, this jotting the leaded shade of smarting smoke and ashes
    below.

Little India

The frazzled stationmaster in his shabby British excuse
    for a uniform shoos away the hoi polloi. His gesture
is surely a tic of the Crown raj who willed this wonder,
    coupled with its compartments of class, a system
that's peanuts compared to the native one of caste,
    as impossible to grasp as the rupee notes are now
for the begging leprous child with stumped hands. Leper,
    the poor foreigner who throws the pittance at your feet
is too repelled to risk brushing you, even as chagrin
    flushes his face. He muses how you can't even raise
a few rupees sewing for chainstores on our side of the globe
    and brushes such thoughts under the carpet
of his scruples. Child, it's true I'm the stumped
    angrezi who cast the sorry note and forgot you.

The Emerald Isle, Sri Lanka

The machine-gun police chat at the temple's checkpoint,
    showered by blood drops of bougainvillea,
common here as deora dé, fuchsia, on our drop in the ocean.

They point out a lizard basking in the foetor along
    the banks of Kandy's lake, where men
were once staked to its floor for speaking out.

The monitor's charcoal body is patterned with links
    as if local gods chained the creature
into itself for some accurst, centuries-old aberration.

When these oddly convivial guards tell us that magic
    words flow from the mouth of
whoever touches the lizard's tongue, I could risk prayer

at the moated temple, not for the gift of words for myself,
    but that the Tamils and
Sinhalese would risk talk, dumb and green as it sounds.

And fancying they've touched the flickering, forked tongue,
    this chevron of evil
would fan out into a spreading sign of peace.

Ululu

After the crossfire of words we lay in bed under cover of dark.
I think you dropped into an obliterating sleep. Hearing the strange
    banshee sound
—a curious mixture of a crying cat and the keen of a loon—
I figured it must be the monkey of these parts you told me of.
It had to be trapped and hurt, perhaps in its final throes.
Asleep, I dreamed my body was washed up by the ocean's procession
    of waves I'd lost myself in
after our latest tempest, and my soul had entered this creature
    high in the trees, ululating to the emptiness of the night.

The Stilt Fisherman

How glad I am
to have come to this out-of-the-way island
—ditching the hubbub of the city
with its pubs and cafés and my literati buddies—
seeking enlightenment by way of a woman.

And even if that's out of the question,
even if we can't know the world through each other,
going our separate ways, I understand why
Muslim sailors called this the Isle of Serendip
as I come upon a stilt fisherman
simply clad in a white lungi
sitting on the perch of his stilt,
steadfast among the breakers.

*

He swings the lasso of his line
and waves me away as I swim to him,
scaring off the fish, buoyant in my stupidity.

*

Now he winds in a shimmering seerfish
and dunks it into his stilt's mesh bag.
He gives thanks and asks forgiveness of the seer.
The ocean in the swell of a wave
washes in around him.

*

I too am supplicant,
having wasted so much time,
all my life it seems,
fishing to be known.
Combers furl and fall
around him, the boom
of tall drums played in the temple
by bowing, anonymous men.

The Malayalam Box

to Gerry Murphy and Gregory O'Donoghue

There we were, ensconced in Bewley's, that's as out of place
    in our city as I am now ferrying in a bockety boat
from Alleppey to Quilon, through a razzle-dazzle
    of lagoons and lakes, in the Cork and Kerry of India.
But such oddity is nothing next to our café's confab,
    impossible to catch as the shiny spray from the prow.
Secured with ballast of repartee, we drifted past murky,
    shallow waters of literary knawvshawl and found ourselves
navigating a course I can't recall we ever traversed.
    Some shelf beneath the lagoons and canals of chat
washed away and the current carried us headlong
    immediately Gerry mentioned some artist's postmortem
about how Seán's heart couldn't negotiate the crosscurrents
    of perfection of the life and of the work.
We gave such notions the kibosh, retorting that what stopped
    our friend's, the scald's ticker
was simply the hole in the heart he happened to be born with.

*

The boathands chitchat among themselves in Malayalam.
    They point to where the bard, Kumaran, drowned
off his boat, reminding me of Tomás Rua. He lost his books
    in a ferry sinking off Derrynane, but saved himself.
We too want to save ourselves and write the dán of life,
    endurance and muted celebration; poetry and life
a kind of palindrome of one another like the word *Malayalam*.

*

We jawed about how poesy has turned in on itself, man-trapped
        like the mongoose that gnawed away at its own hind legs
to slip the trap's jaws, but whether it survives, after dragging
        itself into mangroves, I can't say. A boat glides by.
All-on-board wave. Why is it people on boats wave
        when minutes later, if they passed on the street, they'd not
give each other the time of day? Maybe it's merely that we all
        navigate the same waterway along with the security
of separateness. Is that all a poem is, a wave from a boat?
        Maybe. I'm waving now from my frail, rocky craft.
Can you see me? If I pass on the street later without a nod,
        take no offence. Is that you waving from a passing raft?

*

I signal to you how I want to uncork this corker day.
        You should have seen the teal sheen of the kingfisher;
the boats, not unlike our coracles, laden with copra;
        the fish owl miming stillness; the hammer & sickle flags
traipsed from huts—how they're linked to Vishnu somehow
        in my nudge; how every-blessèd-thing is somehow
threaded together in a homespun stitch; how local bards explain
        Malayalam is a box of various petals: lotus, frangipani,
cosmos . . . how any movement alters the words; how I shake
        these petals for you now out of my own Malayalam box.

17

Pathetic Fallacy

In a villa high in the hill country
I struggle to find a comfortable position
in one of those old, heavy deckchairs
with a real wooden frame and striped canvas
that opens and closes out of and into itself.
It hammocks my body as the trees
sway in and out of each other,
moved by what my Sinhalese waiter calls
the invisible hand of Maruti himself,
fanning the valley all the way
past Shiva's Spear and Ravana's Falls,
past the squat tea bushes and the Tamil women
picking leaves for the teapots of Europe,
past lounging monkeys, past
the paddy terraces
rising in green tiers to the sky.

*

Now a woman walks against the god of the wind.
Maruti opens a space for her.
She moves away from me,
wanting to be alone,
wanting what she calls her space,
aware of my awkwardness, and her own,
away from what earlier was grace
between us, but who can stay at home
with anything for long?

Now she's just looking to be graceful
by herself. I wish her well.

                    *

The wind mimics the sound of falling
water in the leaves,
the sound of Ravana's Falls
where the woman and I mimed the trees earlier—
the world is all intimation of sameness
simultaneously defining continual difference.
The wind and trees susurrus shhh

The Traveling Monk

The Buddhist monk in the saffron robe
goes all his life without a woman.
The marigold monk calls this his destiny.
At last I see, traveling by rickety train
through the deep hill country
of paddy fields and lush tea plantations
with a woman who loves me sometimes
and sometimes puts up with me gladly,
that this might be my destiny:
that I'm a holy man, a bhikku of sorts,
one of the chosen weak, one of the oh so lucky.

The Palindrome Stitch

Now quiet is everything. In your element, you sew a hem, satisfied
    you do something
as you do nothing, like myself doodling this, for once not angling
    for the great poem. A fly alights
on my left hand, then reappears, wearily checking the sand round
    my feet that's so fine it might be gold dust.
A bee must think my head, just washed in honeysuckle shampoo, is
    a flower.
The fly and the bee have fallen for me, and you too by the way
    you glance
in my direction. We're all lulled by the laid-back, jazzy soul
    singer inside our tape recorder
crooning to some woman he's in love with as the palm trees
    are with the sun,
stretching long necks to light, swaying in time with the sea
    and your sewing hand.
They could be the spines of local dancers. There's ease on your
    brow. I say nothing. Everything is quiet now.

The Gecko and Vasco da Gama

The tangerine sun drops into the Arabian Sea. The fishing boats with skis on one side are one-legged catamarans. Fruits bend the branches with luxuriant weight, pineapple and banana especially. Geckos play who-can-stay-still-the-longest on trees I can't name. How strange. How odd we are to each other, and after all these years. Boats settle down to fish for the night under tilly lamps defining darkness. The town lights of Vasco da Gama off along the Indian coast glimmer like the portholes of a great ship that's docked for a long stay, probably for some mending work, allowing sailors shore-leave to become familiar again with their wives, their families, their aloneness. We'll stop here a while.

Behold the Brahmany Kite

That the Brahmany Kite shares the name of a god is not improper
with its rufous body the tincture of Varkala's cliffs and white head
    matching the combers.
The kite riffs, banks and spirals; flapping black-tipped wings
that are mighty as the wings of the skate who might be the bird's
    shade in the stilly water.
The Brahmany makes light of the wind and circles the distant salt-
    and-pepper minarets of Odaayam Mosque
rising above the palms and the silence-made-susurrus of the
    Lakshadweep Sea.
Now the kite is a silhouette in the glare of the sun, reminding me of
    vultures
above the hidden Towers of Silence that Patti and I spotted from the
    Hanging Gardens.
They dined off the cadavers of followers of Zarathustra himself.
And in my way I too believe in the kusthi—the sacred thread—of the
    elements
stitching us all together, and would rather the kite pluck the flesh
    from my bones
than I be laid in the dolled-up box of the West. When the time
    comes, imagine me the grub of the Brahmany.
Keep your elegy eye on the bird a day or so. Watch the kite make
    nothing of me.
Then, as I have now, give the Brahmany an almost imperceptible nod
    and turn and go.

Prayer to Saint Blaise

The Buddhist monks are up chanting and pounding their two-sided
    drums.
They've been at it since before dawn across the sanctuary
    of the lake
in the Temple of the Sacred Tooth, praying to the molar
    of Buddha.
Lately I find myself mumbling a Hail Mary or Our Father on the
    quiet
as I did in the old short-pants days when I thought I was a goner if I
    missed spelling,
was late for school or confessed to impure thoughts about the Clark
    sisters, but now
I'm in trouble deep and childhood's terrors can't hold a candle to
    it. What matter
what the trouble is. We all know trouble—the royal trouble.
    The candle of middle age gutters down
into a malaise of disappointment about the whole hocus-pocus,
    holus-bolus ball of wax, even poesy—
I've lingered too long in the underworld of the poetry circle, another
    jostling jongleur jockeying to sup
from the blood of fame, or rather the ketchup, my ailing throat
    desperate to be heard.

*

Now I swear I'll beeline to the Holy Trinity or whatever chapel
    when I'm back in the country of churches.

I'll not care a damn if any bookish crony spots me dip my hand in the
       font
as I slip inside to kneel among the head-scarved women lighting
       votive candles,
beseeching their special saint for whatever ordinary miracles.

I will light a candle at some saint's side altar, Saint Blaise
       preferably.
Around his feast day I'll queue up for the X of a pair of crossed
       candles to wax my throat
in the hands of a priest lisping the Latin blessing that my voice box
       not fail.
Sound. I'll chance this. I'll come again to poetry pax. I'll kneel before
       my childhood's sacred tooth.

The Nuptial Fish

I thought the minnow was merely a turquoise flick

        but after shadowing it in
                and out of coral
I saw that the greater body
        of the creature below the dorsal fin
                is all
        but invisible most of the time, camouflaged,
flickering in & out of daily life. Look, see

The Family Man and the Rake

I'm like a character in a movie with a doppelgänger
    carrying on with some looker, promising to ditch my family,
but for the kids' sake the affair must be undercover,
    though he can't help parading her at the office party.
She falls for his "you say that to all the girls" poppycock
    and sometimes he falls for it too, taking a last quaff
of wine as he glances furtively at her bedside clock
    before jumping in the shower to wash her scent off.
On the dash home he runs a red light and wonders
    if it's an omen, slipping eternity back on his finger.
He swears, arriving once more to his dinner-in-cinders,
    he was delayed at work, and breaks news of another
business trip; how the job has him too worn out to row.
    You know the story. And at this stage nobody can tell
who's the doppelgänger and who's the doppelgänger's doppel
    in a hall of mirrors, or which one is writing this now.

The Phone Bird

For days I've stayed within range of the phone,
    tethered to my need the way the phone is tethered
        to itself. Some days I listen so hard
            I'm sure I hear it ring.
When anyone calls, they're dumbstruck
    as my shaky greeting turns to despondency.
I admit that if you rang there'd be times
    you'd get an earful for not ringing.
        You know how I brood, turned in
on myself, willing the snake-coiled phone to ring,
    the handset clamped like devouring jaws on the rest.
Now the phone's a sleeping bird with its head tucked
    back in its wing. If you call,
I'll unfurl its neck and tenderly, tenderly I'll sing.

Raising a Glass

The hummingbird
pokes its beak
into diverse flowers,
all with women's names.
How right it is they should
be named after flowers, or
is it the other way round?
What time and country is it?
    You pass me the stem
        of a blossom of white wine
        and laugh and say I have
                a wandering eye for flowers
        like the hummingbird.
        But you're not annoyed.
    You know I'm loopy about women
and love even those called beautiful.
What time or country is that?
I raise my glass to you
without a word, and think
how soon I'll dip my head
between your stems
and mime the
hummingbird.

The Husband's Aubade

There's nothing worse than such ardor so early.
You slip out of bed at cock-crow especially
to sneak in your daily worth of alone time.
My dawn dame, you ride roughshod round our home
as I ease into the jittery nervous system of the day,
with your get-up-and-go bathroom horseplay,
your soprano accompaniment to every chore.

Call the marriage union. I can't take no more.
I'm throwing in the conjugal towel. I'm all vowed out,
running on nuptial empty.
                                    There's no need to pout.
If you weren't about, I'd miss your roughhousing,
your kitchen high jinks, your chirpy singing.
But, love, my early-morning bird of a wife,
you should hightail it now if you value your life.

The Bindi Mirror

The small patch which a married woman places on her fore-head is known as a bindi ('zero'). These are usually bought ready-made from the market and have become almost a fash-ion accessory, with every imaginable shape and colour to match the occasion. You'll also come across a wide variety of used bindis stuck around the mirrors in hotel bathrooms!

—*India*, Lonely Planet Travel Survival Kit

Here we are, ringed by the circular mirror, you in front,
    head bowed, brushing rats' nests and static
in hair that's the long sable-silk of Indian women.
    We're oblivious of each other in that married way
that some call oneness, others call blindness. Your O
    snaps us out of our morning motions
as you spot the various bindis round our mirror.
    The index finger of your wedding-band hand traces
from one to another, connecting confetti zeros
    that are red as the razor-nick on my Adam's apple;
others are inlaid with pearls as if with love itself.
    Who wore that God's teardrop, that bloody arrowhead,
or those joyful signposts, gay-coloured as saris?
    O women of such third eyes, did any of you grow
weary of the SOLD stickers on your brows, the zeros
    of your vows? While your men slept, did you vanish
into the immense Ravana dark of the Indian night?
    Could you have slipped them off like wedding rings
in hotels on our side of the faithless globe?
    Below our moving reflection are rows
of crimson bindis like tiers of shimmering votive flames.

White Worry

He mentioned his box of white noise, how
    he turns on this constant low-level static
to drown out local fighter jets on maneuver, the news
    channel permanently on next door, the snarl
of the chainsaw devouring the sometime forest
    now become a wood closing on our back gardens,
the siren and hooting street traffic; all the rest
    of the relentless, varying normal din.
At first, I thought how superfluous, how modern
    such contraptions are, but who am I to talk?
Look how I rely on low-level worries: the phone bill,
    a snub, something I ought to have said—
all my dear white noise switched habitually on,
    the reliable buzz shrouding our daily black noise.

International Call

A hand holds a receiver out a top-storey window
in a darkening city. The phone is the black
old heavy type. From outside
what can we make of such an event?
The hand, which seems to be a woman's,
holds the phone away from her lover, refusing
to let him answer his high-powered business call.
More likely a mother has got one more
sky-high phone bill and in a tantrum warns
her phone-happy son she'll toss the contraption.
A demented widow, having cracked the number
to the afterlife, holds the receiver out
for the ghost of her lately deceased husband.
He's weary of heaven and wants to hear dusk birds,
particularly the excited choir of city starlings.
It's always dusk now, but the receiver isn't held out
to listen to the birds of the Earth from Heaven.
It's the black ear and mouth in the hand of a woman
as she asks her emigrated sisters and brothers
in a distant country if they can hear the strafing,
and those muffled thuds, how the last thud
made nothing of the hospital where they were slapped
into life. The hand withdraws. The window bangs closed.
The city is shut out. Inside now, the replaced phone
represses a moan. Its ear to the cradle
listens for something approaching from far off.

The Leper and Civil Disobedience

However, Lommán, a very arrogant leper, at the devil's instigation,
was for refusing Bridget's food as usual unless Bridget gave him the
spear of the aforesaid king who had gone home early that morning. . . .
Then Saint Bridget and everybody asked him to eat but to no avail.
Bridget also refused to take food until the high-handed leper ate.

—"Vita Prima Sanctae Brigitae"

Would I were that pain in the ass, incorrigible leper
    egged on, they say, by the devil, to test Saint Bridget.
She couldn't be seen to turn this sorry beggar away.
    In accordance with etiquette, nobody
could touch a crumb. You can imagine the curses
    of diplomats, wives, officers, back-stabbers, holy men
round the hobnobbing table. Bridget bade horsemen gallop
    after the king, to the assembly's gall, the food going cold.
But Bridge had a trick up her saint's sleeve,
    casting a spell that as much as the king and army
seemed to ride away, they'd not journey beyond the gates,
    towing all the paraded weaponry the saint blessed earlier.
The messengers, surprised to reach the troops so soon,
    related the holy woman's request. His majesty declared:
"If Bridget asked for all our arms, I'd obey."
    The couriers returned before the curses were barely uttered.
Everyone tucked into the steaming grub, cold-shouldering
    Lommán as poetasters read ass-licking rhymes and fools
flattered the notables, the powers that be, with mocking jokes.
    All considered themselves noble for taking wisecracks on king,
country and themselves, laughing off vague discomfort.
    As usual actors and singers nudged each other for the limelight.

Town criers chronicled the night, who wore what and so on.

The king riding away through the night smirked to himself,
dying to test his stockpile of new model spears.

Bridget, playing hostess, wore a forlorn smile, avoiding
the eyes of Lommán with his loathsome leprous head in the clouds.

Lommán, feeling a clown, heard snickers aimed his way,
suppressed a frown and smiled at the token victory, focusing on

how many mouths the spear would feed once melted down.

Heron and Li Po on the Blackwater

In an old wooden boat we motor up the Blackwater
that's now a Chinese river, what with the silt-jade water,
    pine and fir cliffs rising on either side, the heron
defining stillness along the banks of yellow iris,
    the odd thatched house, five men's lightning Cork talk,
and my hangover worthy of Li Po. Even being hungover—a word
    that must derive from a Chinese poet's name—is a boon,
having last night burnt off rogue energy without ado.
    Liam Ó and I talk poetry. We could talk poetry blue
in the face. We'll miss such gab soon enough.
    At the tiller now, he negotiates shallow waters. We go
river-quiet and drift off into ourselves. I snag
    in the weeds of worry and settle on how I fault Patti,
exaggerating so-called flaws in the conjugal hall of mirrors,
    how say, a dress doesn't suit; how I always keep an eye
cocked for the perfect woman, Li Po's girl of Yueh, conjured
    yesterday by the Yangtze Take-Away on Evergreen Street.
The heron undoes its wings. I recall the story about this guy
    who stumbles on a hurt heron. He nurses her well.
In gratitude, even love, she returns to him
    in the guise of his dream girl of Yueh, settling
with him for good provided he stays out of her room.
    Everything's hunkydory till one day he can't resist
sneaking in, to discover the heron. On seeing his glare
    accuse her that she's an illusion, the bird flies away.

It took all this time for the old story to hit home. I yak
about this or that till we row into dock. Our oars
are wings. Patti's come down to meet us. I spot her on
the leeward shore. We wave to one another.

The Speakeasy Oath

to Liam Ó Muirthile

You borrowed my kimono with Japanese prints and verse legends of
    the soul's struggles,
its script more readable than the serif characters of our tattered Irish
    primers.
As you boiled water for the magic brew of Barry's tea, the Cork
    ginseng, to kick-start the day,
the kimono's druid sleeves, trailing across the stove, hey-presto
    caught fire.

Being still out for the count, I was startled awake by you raising the
    roof, ullagoning,
having a conniption, a canary, bellising *Táim trí thine, Fuck,*
    Brostaigh, Bollox,
and a veritable string of swear words right out of the lost lexicon of
    old Irish oaths.
I vaulted out and tore into the kitchen without a stitch on.
    You were berilling
and back-berilling, in a mighty footer, like some stepdancer
    gone bonkers, lepping out a new berserk dance.

I got into the act, an bhriogáid dóiteáin, flaking the flaming sleeve,
    dousing
us pair of prancing artists with the kettle's hot water; me in
    me scald, dancing buff;
my willy, micky, connihaly, langer, crown jewels, one-eyed baldy
    man, thingamajig

keeping time to the fire jig. We fell on the floor in stitches.
    A chara,
you yammered in between guffaws that it was a sign, a
       thumbs-up from the muses,
after our night before's oath to set the poetry world on fire while
       Big Joe Burrell, an fear gorm, blithely blues-sang.

Your Irish and my darned Cork-English airishin dipped and rose
       like the smoke in the yuppy Dockside,
the closest we could get to our mythical speakeasy with the New
       York mountains
across the lake leapfrogging each other into the dark eternity of
       America.

Tagging the Stealer

to David Cavanagh

So much of it I hadn't a bull's notion of
and like the usual ignoramus who casts his eyes
at, say, a Jackson Pollock or "This Is Just to Say,"
I scoffed at it. I didn't twig how it was as close
to art as art itself with its pregame ballyhoo,
antics, rhubarbs, scheming, luck; its look
as if little or nothing is going on.
How often have we waited for the magic
in the hands of some flipper throwing a slider,
sinker, knuckler, jug-handle, submarine or screwball?
If we're lucky, the slugger hits a daisy cutter
with a choke-up or connects with a Baltimore chop
and a ball hawk catches a can of corn
with a basket catch and the ball rounds the horn—
Oh, look, Davo, how I'm sent sailing
right out of the ball park just by its lingo.
But I swear the most memorable play I witnessed
was with you on our highstools in the Daily Planet
as we slugged our Saturday night elixirs.
The Yankees were playing your Toronto Blue Jays.
They were tied at the top of the 9th.
I can't now for the life of me remember
who won, nor the name of the catcher, except
he was an unknown, yet no rookie.
Suddenly behind the pinch hitter's back he signaled
the pitcher, though no one copped until seconds later
as the catcher fireballed the potato to the first baseman,

40

tagging the stealer. It doesn't sound like much,
but everyone stood up round the house Ruth built
like hairs on the back of the neck, because the magic
was scary too. Jesus, give each of us just once
a poem the equal of that unknown man's talking hand.

To Frank O'Hara

Along the Avenue of the Americas dudes shoot the breeze,
        dribbling the globe of a basketball, ballhopping each other
or whatever's the New York for slag, greg and razz.
        Honking taxis, common as cockroaches here, helter-
skelter as if the light was just flipped. The light's always
        just flipped in this off-its-rocker city. Frank,
the neon's still frankly heartbreaking on sunny days.
        A gay couple, pinup boys, schmooze and happy talk
their way downtown as traffic signals flip green
        all up the infinity of the avenue. Frankie boy,
New York is lonely without you. Come back. Lean
        on your elbow; take in agitating rap guys
mouthing words now that say the reverse like bad and mean.
        Manhattan's still mean, Frank. You're bad. Where ya been?

The Memory Quilt

to Mona Phillips, dying

Ah my Yankee Doodle Dandess grandma, I promised you
    this crochet of words a decade
        and a day ago. Have I, Tailor Tardy, left it too
late? Your presence here ends, to fade
    and tear. Let's call an ace a spade
        and admit, our old card-playing Baptist
seamstress, that you are already badly missed,
        being here and not here, our grief patched to
your absence with that blind stitch
    you showed distaff daughter and granddaughter. Do you
        hear me? Am I dropping the stitch?
            Christ, this craft's a bitch.
Excuse me language, Mona,
    my fustian transmutation of your domestic art. Nana,
where are you off to now? Be sure to say hello
    to my Da. The first one's on me. Tell him
watch the spirits. Spirits? Cheers. You'll know
    him by yours truly. Yodel an old Baptist hymn.
He likes a song. Rob too. Patti jokes that you'll find them
    two in the great smoking room of heaven.
Hobble them up a few earthly smokes from the 7-Eleven.

            *

You know, often when our home's Vermont-chilly,
    I wrap, without thinking, your quilt around me—
        the quilt with your family's history
    that you outlined in the plain calico hands of Patti,

Rob, Lois, Russell and all the other hands.
Each is stitched into the palmistry of muslin squares.
    Certain life-line strands
                unravel and the hands tear.
    You wave goodbye
                from the embroidered emblems around
        yours and the other hands, the simplifying background
of each life: your sewing box, Rob's saw, Lo's threaded eye,
John's lost specs, Russ's firehat. . . . Ah Mona hardbye hardbye.

The Blind Stitch

I can't say why rightly, but suddenly it's clear once more
    what holds us together as we sit, recumbent in the old ease
of each other's company, chewing the rag about friends,
    a poem we loved and such-like. Your Portuguese skin,
set off by a turquoise dress, doesn't hinder either.
    But there's something more than tan-deep between us.
I sew a button to a waistcoat you made me, ravelled years ago.
    You hemmed it with the stitch you mend a frock with now.
Our hands, without thought for individual movement, sew in
    and out, entering and leaving at one and the same time.
If truth be told, the thread had frayed between us, unnoticed,
    except for the odd rip. But as we sew, love is
in the mending, and though nothing's said, we feel it
    in a lightness of mood, our ease, our blind stitch.

Lepers' Walk

We're away for slates, secure in the signifying gatch
of our city, gabbing about spotting the talent
along the meandering, quondam river of Patrick Street.
At the disco, if the gauzer stayed past the clinger,
the fella held off till the second date and all clear
of heavy breathing to slip the hand under a blouse
along the crepuscular Lee fields, Lough, or Lovers' Walk
that's the epitome of a lovers' walk. This winding incline
skirts the city, bordered with necking nooks and arbours.

Having long since chucked testing such love,
doing a line now with your ersatz crush, Madam Words,
you switch to tell us with a lover's ardour how Lovers' Walk
was Siúl na Lobhar in the Gaelic days, but the Sasanach,
anglicizing street names, mistook the *bh* Irish v sound.
Then maybe cúpla jorums too many, feeling jilted
by our city that you still can't let go, you turn inward.
You fume in a shamanistic fury about how lepers
had to steal to the contagion hospital up this hill.
They bypassed locals, themselves infected
with the typical small-town *Mycobacterium leprae*,
the paralysis that no soul dare attempt anything
different, diagnosed as rising above one's station.
Whether you're right or no, for you I'd have the city
ring the bells of its malady, cleansing itself
in admission.
                    And there are other unforeseen hybrids

rampant on the islands of Academe and Literati.
We stepped onto these shores with such expectation
of goodwill and safety, certain the vaccine of these
learnèd isles would protect inhabitants from sickness,
only to find strains not unlike the small-town class: fear
of other island enclaves, numb envy
among locals, immunity to the very spirit-vaccine
they themselves dose out. How can we escape
who must be infected now too? Is there a raft,
camouflaged among palms along the patrolled banks,
that some cloudless night we can sally forth upon?
We'd raise the tattered sails of learning and be borne
on a kindly, out-of-the-dark zephyr away, guiding ourselves
by the night sky of humility, itself the journey's end.
My friend, for what else did we come all this way?